A Book of
Kisses

kiss (kis), _v._ [ME _kissen_, fr. OE _cyssan_; akin to OHG _kussen_ to kiss]: to touch with the lips, especially as a sign of affection and a nifty way to say hello.

Syn buss, osculate, lip, peck, smack, smooch, [obs.] smouch

kiss, n. a caress with the lips.
kissable, adj. someone or
something worthy of kissing.
Ant unkissable

For Kaitlyn and Tara, with Father Kisses!

—D.R.

For Scott, my handsome prince, with love and kisses.

—L.R.

A Book of Kisses

by Dave Ross

illustrated by Laura Rader

SCHOLASTIC INC.

New York Toronto London Auckland Sydney
Mexico City New Delhi Hong Kong

ISBN 0-439-20860-2

Text copyright © 2000 by Dave Ross.
Illustrations copyright © 2000 by Laura Rader.
All rights reserved.
Published by Scholastic Inc., 555 Broadway, New York, NY 10012,
by arrangement with HarperCollins Publishers.
SCHOLASTIC and associated logos are trademarks and/or registered
trademarks of Scholastic Inc.

12 11 10 9 8 7 6 5 4 3 2   1 2 3 4 5 6/0

Printed in the U.S.A.   14

First Scholastic printing, January 2001

Typography by Al Cetta

There are all kinds of kisses in the world . . .

Good Morning Kisses

Going to School Kisses
Sometimes this is called the Kiss-and-Go.

After School Kisses

Sometimes a kiss is better than a snack.

When Mom or Dad Comes Home Kisses

Good Night Kisses

Lots of families also have Getting-into-Bed Kisses,

Bedtime Story Kisses,
and
Turning-Out-the-Light
Kisses.

There are kisses for when you come and go.
Hello Kisses

Good-bye Kisses
In some countries, these are Double Cheek Kisses.

Bon Voyage Kisses

Wave from the Car Kisses
Also known as Smeary Window Kisses.

There are kisses that make you feel better.

Boo-boo Kisses

Sick-in-Bed Kisses
Sometimes these lead
to
Doctor Visit Kisses.

I'm Sorry Kisses

Often the best way to end an argument is with a kiss.

But a handshake will do, too!

There are kisses for special occasions.

Good Report Card Kisses

Winning Kisses

Congratulations Kisses

Valentine Kisses

Birthday Kisses

These only come around once a year,
so make the most of them!

And, of course, there are Family Kisses.

Sometimes called an Assembly Line Kiss in large families.

Family Kisses include:
Mom and Dad Kisses

Grandma and Grandpa Kisses

Great-Uncle Fred Kisses
Watch out for the whiskers!

Brother and Sister Kisses
Otherwise known as "Ew Yuck!" Kisses.

Short or tall, near or far, there are as many ways of kissing as there are different kinds of people.

Promise Kisses

First make a promise.

Then kiss your pinky.

Touch pinkies.

Now you've made a promise kiss!

Just remember to keep it.

Tiptoe Kisses
  Useful for small children.

Forehead Kisses
Used frequently by tall people.

Nose and Toes Kisses

Tummy Kisses

Sometimes called a Raspberry Kiss.

Butterfly Kisses

Bat your eyelashes against someone's cheek—that's a Butterfly Kiss!

Underwater Kisses

Remember to breathe out!

Rubbing Noses Kisses

These can keep you warm on cold days!

Bubble Gum Kisses

Caution, you can get stuck on these kisses.

Candy Kisses
are very sweet.

Princess Kisses

Perfect for greeting a princess, but not very nice
if her hands are unwashed!

Prince Kisses

You may have to kiss a lot of frogs

before you find the handsome prince.

A kiss is an easy way
to remind someone you care.

Kisses can be given
anytime, anywhere.

If kisses are given with love and respect, they turn a rotten day into a great day.

All kisses say special things,

but the most special thing a kiss can say is "I Love You."

Kisses from Around the World